Cyber Security 2025 Trends

About
With over 23 years of dedicated service in the field of cyber security, this author combines a distinguished background as a veteran of the UK Armed Forces with extensive experience in safeguarding digital landscapes. Their tenure includes significant contributions to both local and central government departments, where they have provided exceptional cyber security solutions. Known for their ability to demystify complex concepts, they leverage a unique blend of military discipline and industry expertise, establishing themselves as a formidable authority in the realm of cyber security.

Table of Contents

6. Internet of Things (IoT) Security Challenges

7. Cybersecurity in the Age of Quantum Computing

8. Privacy Enhancements and Personal Data Protection

9. Cybersecurity Culture and Awareness

10. Incident Response and Recovery Trends

1. The Evolving Threat Landscape

1.1 Rise of Advanced Persistent Threats (APTs)

Advanced Persistent Threats (APTs) are complex, sophisticated cyber threats that infiltrate networks with the specific aim of stealing data or compromising sensitive information over an extended period. Unlike traditional cyber attacks, which are generally opportunistic and hit-and-run in nature, APTs are characterized by their calculated approach and sustained efforts. Attackers behind APTs often take immense time to plan their infiltration, using a combination of social engineering, malware, and zero-day exploits to gain access to target environments. Once inside, they maintain a presence undetected for weeks, months, or even years, establishing themselves in the victim's network to carry out their objectives while remaining hidden from standard security measures. This stealthy persistence allows attackers to exfiltrate data methodically, often bypassing detection systems designed to thwart less sophisticated threats.

Understanding the implications of APTs for cybersecurity is crucial. Organizations must prioritize advanced security solutions and continuous monitoring to defend against these threats. Traditional defenses, such as simple firewalls and antivirus programs, are often inadequate. Cybersecurity professionals must adopt a proactive approach encompassing threat intelligence, user training, and incident response planning. Rather than merely reacting to breaches, there is a pressing need to develop comprehensive strategies that anticipate breaches and strengthen organizational resilience by incorporating behavioural analysis and anomaly detection technologies. Only through such preparations can organizations hope to safeguard their sensitive information from this ever-evolving threat landscape.

To grasp the current nature of APTs, it is essential to examine their historical context. One of the earliest recognized APT incidents was the breach of the U.S. Department of Energy in the late 1990s, often attributed to state-sponsored actors. This incident set a precedent for the kinds of sustained, targeted attacks that would proliferate in the following decades. As the internet evolved, so did the tactics employed by APT groups. The infamous Stuxnet worm, discovered in 2010, showcased how APTs could not only exfiltrate data but also cause physical damage, targeting industrial control systems to disrupt critical infrastructure. Such examples demonstrate a pivotal shift from information theft to potential disruption, raising alarms on the vulnerabilities of essential services.

In subsequent years, incidents like the 2014 Sony Pictures hack and the 2016 U.S. presidential election interference illustrated the range of motivations driving APTs, from corporate espionage to political influence. As APT tactics continue to evolve, their reliance on cyber-espionage and strategic disinformation campaigns has become pronounced, emphasizing the need for organizations to develop intelligence capabilities that go beyond traditional defenses. The continual evolution of these threats calls for cybersecurity professionals to stay informed on emerging tactics and to leverage adaptive defense mechanisms that can mitigate potential APT impacts. Regularly updating incident response plans and threat intelligence databases is not just beneficial but necessary in this relentless battle against advanced persistent threats.

Staying ahead in the battle against APTs is crucial for security teams. Regularly conducting threat assessments, investing in updated technology, and engaging in continuous training for staff can help organizations remain resilient in the face of evolving tactics. Building a culture of security awareness and vigilance is key in defending against the silent infiltrators that characterize APTs.

1.2 The Surge in Ransomware Attacks

Current trends indicate a significant rise in ransomware incidents, with attacks becoming more sophisticated and widespread. Organizations across various sectors are feeling the pressure as cybercriminals increasingly exploit vulnerabilities in digital infrastructures. This surge can be attributed to several factors, including the growing reliance on remote working environments, increasing use of cloud-based solutions, and the proliferation of Internet of Things (IoT) devices. As organizations adopt more connected technologies, the attack surface expands, making them more attractive targets for ransomware attacks. The impact on organizations has been profound, both financially and operationally. Many companies face not only the immediate cost of ransom payments but also long-term repercussions such as loss of customer trust, potential legal consequences, and disruptions to business operations.

To counter the rise of ransomware, organizations must implement effective defensive strategies that go beyond traditional security measures. A multi-layered security approach is essential, combining advanced technologies like endpoint detection and response (EDR) with regular employee training programs that focus on recognizing phishing attempts and other social engineering tactics. Regularly updating and patching software across all systems is crucial to eliminate known vulnerabilities that can be exploited by attackers. Incident response plans should also be in place, allowing organizations to respond quickly and efficiently to ransomware incidents, minimizing damage and restoring operations. Backing up data regularly and ensuring that backup systems are not directly accessible from the network can mitigate the impact of successful ransomware attacks.

Staying ahead of ransomware threats will require organizations to continually adapt their defensive postures as cybercriminal techniques evolve. Engaging in threat intelligence sharing with other entities can provide valuable insights into emerging threats and effective countermeasures. Fostering a culture of cybersecurity awareness at all levels of the organization ensures that everyone is vigilant and understands their role in protecting enterprise assets. One practical tip is to conduct simulated attacks to test the readiness of your organization against ransomware, ensuring that teams are prepared to handle real-life scenarios effectively.

1.3 Growing Concerns over State-Sponsored Cyber Activities

State-sponsored cyber activities represent a multifaceted spectrum of threats that have evolved dramatically in recent years. These activities often encompass cyber espionage, where nation-states seek to gather intelligence by infiltrating networks of foreign governments or corporations. Another common type is cyber warfare, which involves the deployment of harmful cyber operations designed to disrupt critical infrastructure. Examples include attacks on energy grids and financial institutions, aiming to sow chaos or test the resilience of a target country's systems. Additionally, we now see a rise in information warfare tactics, where misinformation and disinformation campaigns are conducted to undermine public trust and manipulate social discourse. As these methods become more sophisticated, the stakes for national security and the stability of the global order continue to escalate, prompting urgent discussions among cybersecurity experts and policymakers alike.

The global ramifications of state-sponsored cyber operations are profound and far-reaching. These activities can lead to significant diplomatic tensions, as nations retaliate against perceived cyber aggressions. The erosion of trust between countries is exacerbated, with cyber incidents often fuelling hostility and leading to a cycle of escalation that can spill over into physical confrontations. Moreover, the ramifications are not limited to state actors; private industries often become collateral damage. A single breach can compromise sensitive data, leading to financial loss and reputational harm that resonates across borders. Future trends indicate that as interconnectivity increases, the potential for mass disruption via cyberspace expands exponentially, raising concerns about how nations will navigate these challenges in a world that relies heavily on digital infrastructure.

In this evolving landscape, cybersecurity professionals must prioritize enhancing their defenses against these sophisticated threats. It is crucial to adopt proactive measures, including regular vulnerability assessments and developing comprehensive incident response plans. Strengthening partnerships between public and private sectors can also bolster collective defenses against shared threats. Engaging in tabletop exercises to simulate cyber incidents can prepare teams for real-world scenarios, ensuring they swiftly and effectively mitigate the impact of potential breaches. Given that state-sponsored activities are unlikely to diminish, fostering a culture of cybersecurity awareness is imperative for organizations aiming to secure their networks and information in the years to come.

2. Cloud Security Innovations

2.1 Enhanced Security Postures for Multi-Cloud Environments

Multi-cloud environments present a unique set of security challenges that organizations must navigate. Each cloud provider has its own architecture, security measures, and compliance standards, creating a complex landscape for security professionals. One major issue is the lack of uniformity across platforms. Different configurations can lead to inconsistent application of security policies, making it tougher to monitor and protect data across various environments. Beyond this inconsistency, the challenge of data visibility arises. When data is spread across multiple clouds, determining where sensitive information resides and who has access can be daunting. This opacity increases the risk of breaches and data loss. Additionally, integration issues can create vulnerabilities, with organizations using third-party tools or APIs that may not comply with stringent security norms, inadvertently introducing new points of failure into their systems. Understanding these unique security challenges is vital for effective risk management within multi-cloud architectures.

To counteract the security issues inherent in multi-cloud setups, adopting best practices can significantly strengthen an organization's security posture. First, organizations need to implement a robust identity and access management solution. Centralizing user access across all cloud environments ensures that permissions are properly managed and that users have only the access necessary for their roles.

Multi-factor authentication should also be mandatory, adding an additional layer of security against unauthorized access. Regular audits and assessments are crucial as well. Security professionals should conduct frequent evaluations of security policies and configurations to identify vulnerabilities and enforce compliance with the latest regulations. Additionally, employing comprehensive encryption strategies—both for data at rest and in transit—helps secure sensitive information, regardless of where it resides. Training staff on cloud security best practices is equally important, as human error remains one of the leading causes of security breaches.

Keeping pace with emerging trends in cloud security will further enhance protections. Machine learning and AI technologies are becoming invaluable tools in detecting abnormal patterns and potential threats across multi-cloud environments. By implementing advanced analytics, organizations can gain enhanced visibility into user activity and data flows, enabling quicker response to suspicious activities. As cloud environments evolve, so too should the security strategies that protect them. Continuous adaptation and learning will be essential as threats become more sophisticated. Cybersecurity professionals must stay informed about advancements and review their security measures regularly, integrating innovative tools that can anticipate and respond to new vulnerabilities and attack vectors. Regularly updating and refining an organization's security posture will ensure that defenses remain strong and relevant in this rapidly changing digital landscape.

2.2 Cloud-Native Security Tools for 2025

In the rapidly evolving landscape of cloud computing, numerous security tools have emerged that are tailored specifically for cloud environments. These tools have been designed to address the unique challenges posed by the cloud, such as the distributed nature of applications and the scalability requirements that modern businesses demand. One of the notable advancements is the adoption of artificial intelligence and machine learning in security tools. These technologies enable real-time anomaly detection and predictive analytics, allowing organizations to identify potential threats before they escalate into significant issues. Furthermore, tools that focus on container security have gained prominence as more companies move towards containerized applications. These tools ensure that containers are secure throughout their lifecycle, from development to deployment. Additionally, cloud security posture management tools have become essential, providing continuous compliance monitoring and risk assessment for cloud resources, thus ensuring that organizations adhere to best practices and regulatory requirements in their cloud environments.

Integrating emerging cloud-native security tools into existing security frameworks requires a thoughtful approach to ensure effectiveness and minimize disruptions. A phased implementation strategy is often the most effective method. This begins with a thorough assessment of current security practices and identifying gaps. Understanding the functionalities of these new tools is crucial; conducting pilot programs can help teams evaluate the effectiveness and compatibility of the new tools with existing infrastructure. Collaboration between development and security teams, often referred to as DevSecOps, should be emphasized during the integration process to ensure that security becomes a shared responsibility. Additionally, comprehensive training for staff on the new tools will facilitate smoother transitions and optimize usage. Regular reviews and updates to the security framework are also necessary to accommodate the evolving threat landscape and ensure continued effectiveness. Staying updated with the latest security practices will not only enhance security posture but also instil confidence among stakeholders.

As cyber threats continue to evolve, it is imperative for security professionals to stay ahead by continuously integrating and adapting new tools effectively. An actionable tip is to dedicate specific resources for ongoing security education and training sessions tailored to the new tools being implemented. This will not only improve the overall security culture within the organization but also ensure that every team member is equipped to utilize these tools to their full potential.

2.3 The Impact of Zero Trust Architecture on Cloud Security

The concept of Zero Trust Architecture (ZTA) revolves around a fundamental principle: never trust, always verify. In the context of cloud security, this means that every user, device, and application must be authenticated and authorized before being granted access to critical resources. As organizations increasingly migrate their operations to the cloud, traditional security models, which often rely on the security of the perimeter, become obsolete. Cybersecurity threats are more sophisticated and prevalent than ever, emphasizing the importance of ZTA. Applying these principles in cloud environments can significantly improve a company's security posture by minimizing the attack surface and ensuring that only verified users can access sensitive data. With features like micro-segmentation, granular access controls, and real-time monitoring, Zero Trust helps organizations protect their cloud assets efficiently and effectively, making it a vital approach for current and future security strategies.

Several organizations have successfully implemented Zero Trust models to enhance their cloud security, providing valuable insights for cybersecurity professionals. For instance, a leading financial services firm transitioned to a Zero Trust model that included multifactor authentication and strict identity and access management. This shift not only improved the security of sensitive financial information but also streamlined user experiences across cloud applications. Another example is a major healthcare provider that adopted Zero Trust to safeguard patient data in compliance with HIPAA regulations. By implementing continuous monitoring and robust access policies, the organization was able to significantly reduce data breach incidents while maintaining compliance. These real-world applications highlight how Zero Trust can tackle the unique challenges posed by cloud environments, allowing for a more secure operational framework.

Given the dynamic landscape of cyber threats, implementing Zero Trust is not just a reactive measure; it is an essential strategy for foreseeing potential vulnerabilities and addressing them proactively. For organizations looking to develop a future-proof cloud security strategy, understanding and embracing Zero Trust principles is imperative. Continuous education on emerging threats and regular assessments of security frameworks will keep systems robust and resilient against evolving attacks. As security professionals prepare for the future, keeping abreast of the latest Zero Trust techniques and tools will enhance their capabilities to protect their organization's digital assets.

3. Artificial Intelligence and Machine Learning in Cybersecurity

3.1 AI-Driven Threat Detection Mechanisms

AI algorithms function as advanced analytical tools designed to sift through vast amounts of data, searching for patterns and anomalies that signify potential threats. Machine learning, a subset of AI, employs statistical techniques to enable systems to improve their detection capabilities over time as they are exposed to more data. These algorithms can learn from previous incidents, recognizing the characteristics of attacks such as malware, phishing attempts, and insider threats. By employing techniques such as supervised learning, where models are trained on labeled datasets, and unsupervised learning, where they identify patterns without pre-existing labels, AI can adapt to ever-changing strategies employed by cyber adversaries. Natural language processing (NLP) enables AI to analyze text data, extracting insights from social media, email communications, and other textual sources. This helps in identifying trends in user behaviour or detecting suspicious activities in real-time, minimizing response times and enhancing overall security posture.

The future of AI in cyber security holds immense promise, particularly in the realm of pre-emptive security measures. With advancements in predictive analytics, AI is poised to anticipate potential security breaches before they occur. By utilizing threat intelligence feeds, AI can analyze emerging vulnerabilities and correlate them with specific organizational contexts, allowing for tailored defense strategies. As AI systems become more sophisticated, they will increasingly integrate with existing security frameworks, facilitating a proactive approach to threat management. This synergy will contribute to the automation of routine security tasks, freeing professionals to focus on more strategic initiatives. Moreover, the development of explainable AI is likely to enhance trust among security teams, enabling them to understand the reasoning behind specific threat assessments. As the threat landscape evolves, the ability to adapt quickly and efficiently will rely heavily on the intelligent integration of AI technologies into security protocols.

Staying abreast of these rapidly evolving AI capabilities is essential for cyber security professionals. Engaging with the latest AI tools and exploring opportunities for continuous training in machine learning techniques will provide a competitive edge. Establishing collaborations with AI specialists can foster a deeper understanding of how these technologies can be leveraged effectively in security infrastructures. To ensure a comprehensive defense strategy, organizations should prioritize building a robust data collection framework, supplementing AI predictions with human expertise and oversight, thus creating a resilient security ecosystem.

3.2 The Role of Machine Learning in Predictive Analytics

Machine learning serves as a cornerstone for modern cybersecurity, enabling professionals to analyze vast amounts of data and identify patterns indicative of potential threats. Understanding the foundations of machine learning is essential for cybersecurity experts aiming to leverage these technologies effectively. At its core, machine learning involves algorithms that learn from data, improving their performance over time without explicit programming. In a cybersecurity context, this means developing systems robust enough to detect anomalies by continuously learning from previous attacks and recognizing new forms of them. These systems utilize a variety of algorithms, such as decision trees and neural networks, to classify data and predict future risks. As machine learning technology evolves, its ability to adapt to emerging threats becomes increasingly vital for maintaining secure environments.

Predictive analytics, powered by machine learning, allows cybersecurity professionals to anticipate threats before they materialize. By applying statistical techniques to historical data, machine learning models can create predictive models that highlight vulnerabilities within systems. These models analyze patterns and trends, even in seemingly unrelated data, providing insights that can help pre-empt cyber attacks. For example, by examining user behaviour patterns and system logs, machine learning algorithms can flag abnormal activities that may indicate a breach. Furthermore, as we move toward 2025, the integration of deeper learning techniques will enhance these predictive capabilities, allowing professionals to not only identify vulnerabilities but also simulate potential attack scenarios and develop proactive defenses tailored to specific environments. The future of threat anticipation hinges upon establishing robust predictive models and empowering cybersecurity teams with actionable intelligence.

To maximize the potential of machine learning in predictive analytics, cybersecurity professionals should focus on continuous learning and close collaboration with data scientists. This partnership will ensure that algorithms remain relevant and capable of addressing the ever-evolving landscape of cyber threats. Additionally, investing in higher-quality data for model training will enhance accuracy and reliability, leading to more effective detection and prevention strategies. An often-overlooked but crucial aspect is the importance of ethical considerations and biases in machine learning, which must be addressed to build trustworthy and transparent systems. Emphasizing these elements will not only improve predictive models but also cultivate a security-first mindset across organizations.

3.3 Ethical Considerations of AI in Cyber Threat Mitigation

Organizations increasingly employ artificial intelligence to bolster their cybersecurity defenses, but this reliance introduces complex ethical dilemmas. One major concern involves the potential for biases in AI algorithms. If the data used to train these systems is flawed or unrepresentative, the decisions made by AI could unfairly target specific populations or overlook certain threats. This raises questions about accountability when AI systems misidentify or fail to recognize cyber threats, leading to unjust repercussions and loss of trust among users. Additionally, the use of AI in surveillance poses moral challenges. While tracking particular activities may enhance security, it also risks infringing on privacy rights, leading to a surveillance state where individuals are constantly monitored. Therefore, addressing these moral complexities is paramount to ensure that AI in cybersecurity does not become a tool for oppression or discrimination.

To ethically deploy AI in threat detection and response, organizations must establish clear best practices that prioritize transparency, accountability, and fairness. One essential guideline is to implement robust testing and evaluation phases for AI systems before their full deployment. This includes diverse data sets that reflect a wide range of scenarios to minimize bias. Continuous monitoring of AI systems in real-time is also critical; regular audits can help identify unintentional biases or errors, allowing teams to adjust algorithms accordingly. Furthermore, fostering an ethical culture within cybersecurity teams can enhance awareness of the implications of AI usage. Training professionals to recognize the ethical dimensions of their work will empower them to make informed decisions that align with moral standards. Lastly, collaborating with ethicists and stakeholders can provide valuable insights that shape AI implementations, ensuring they serve the greater good while effectively mitigating cyber threats.

As cybersecurity professionals look to 2025, integrating ethical considerations into AI strategies will not only enhance threat detection but also build public trust. Establishing frameworks that embrace ethical principles fundamentally strengthens cybersecurity posture and aligns with the growing societal demand for accountability. By keeping ethical implications at the forefront of AI development and deployment, organizations can navigate the complex landscape of cyber threats while prioritizing the rights and dignity of every individual.

4. The Future of Cybersecurity Workforce

4.1 The Rise of Cybersecurity Automation

Automation trends in cybersecurity have been on the rise, reflecting a shift toward greater efficiency and responsiveness in an era where cyber threats continually evolve. Organizations are recognizing that manual processes are often too slow to keep pace with the rapid nature of attacks, leading them to adopt automated solutions. These solutions include automated threat detection systems, machine learning algorithms for anomaly detection, and advanced security orchestration tools that streamline incident response. By integrating automation into their frameworks, cybersecurity professionals are not only reducing the time it takes to identify and respond to threats but also minimizing the likelihood of human error. The proliferation of tools that can automatically analyze vast amounts of data and provide actionable insights has transformed the way security teams operate, allowing them to focus on more strategic tasks while relying on automation to manage routine procedures.

Looking to the future, the trajectory of cybersecurity automation suggests an even deeper integration within organizational structures. As the workforce continues to adapt to more sophisticated threats, the role of automation will expand beyond just detection and response. Predictive analytics will play a key part in pre-emptively identifying potential vulnerabilities, enhancing the proactive nature of cybersecurity measures. Furthermore, the interplay between artificial intelligence and machine learning will lead to the development of self-learning systems capable of adapting to new threats without extensive human oversight. This may result in a workforce that is less burdened by repetitive tasks, allowing for higher levels of innovation and creativity in addressing emerging security challenges. However, this transition will also require upskilling professionals who must learn to work alongside these advanced tools effectively.

As organizations embrace these advancements, they should also remain mindful of the implications for workforce dynamics. The integration of automation in cybersecurity is not about replacing human roles but rather augmenting them to enhance overall security posture. Professionals must prepare for a landscape where collaboration with automated systems is the norm. Staying informed about the latest tools and technologies will be essential. Cybersecurity leaders should foster a culture of continuous learning and adaptability, enabling their teams to leverage automation to its fullest potential while maintaining a human touch in strategy and decision-making. Regular training and cross-training between team members on emerging technologies and automated processes can significantly enhance resilience against cyber threats.

4.2 Upskilling and Reskilling Cyber Professionals

Identifying key skill gaps within the current cybersecurity workforce is essential for addressing the rapidly evolving landscape of cyber threats. Many professionals currently in the field lack proficiency in emerging technologies such as artificial intelligence, machine learning, and cloud security. The need for advanced knowledge in threat intelligence, incident response, and data privacy regulations is growing. Additionally, soft skills like communication, teamwork, and critical thinking are often overlooked but equally important in today's collaborative cybersecurity environments. Organizations must regularly assess their teams' capabilities and match them against industry standards to pinpoint these gaps effectively. This requires a comprehensive understanding of not just technical skills but also an awareness of new trends, criminal methodologies, and regulatory changes that can impact cybersecurity strategy.

To effectively upskill and reskill cybersecurity professionals, organizations should consider implementing a variety of training programs tailored to their specific needs and the skill gaps identified. Blended learning approaches that combine online courses, hands-on workshops, and real-world simulations can facilitate deeper learning. Mentorship programs that pair less experienced staff with seasoned professionals can also be invaluable, providing insight and encouragement. Furthermore, companies should invest in continuous learning platforms that offer access to the latest cybersecurity developments, ensuring that employees remain engaged and informed. Regular assessments and certifications can motivate professionals to stay current with their skills and provide tangible proof of their advancements, ensuring their relevance in the rapidly changing field.

As professionals look ahead to 2025, it is crucial to embrace a mindset of lifelong learning. Keeping pace with technological advancements and shifts in the security landscape requires agility and an openness to acquiring new competencies. Engaging with industry groups, attending conferences, and participating in online forums can enrich knowledge and provide essential networking opportunities. Additionally, making time for personal projects or contributing to open-source cybersecurity initiatives can help individuals hone their skills in a practical context, further enhancing their expertise and employment prospects in the ever-competitive job market.

4.3 Diversity and Inclusion in Cybersecurity Roles

The need for diversity in cybersecurity cannot be overstated. Different perspectives enhance problem-solving capabilities, a critical factor in a field that requires constant innovation and adaptation to new threats. Diverse teams bring together unique experiences and viewpoints, enabling them to uncover vulnerabilities and develop more effective security strategies. This variety fosters creativity, allowing for innovative solutions that may not arise within a homogenous group. In a rapidly evolving landscape where cyber threats are increasingly sophisticated, a diverse workforce is essential to ensure that organizations effectively anticipate potential challenges and respond accordingly. As organizations look towards 2025, the importance of diverse voices and backgrounds becomes a necessary element in building resilient cybersecurity strategies that can withstand future challenges.

Implementing strategies to promote diversity and inclusion within cybersecurity teams requires a multifaceted approach. It starts with creating an organizational culture that values and respects differences, encouraging open communication and collaboration among all team members. Recruitment practices should be broadened to reach underrepresented groups, including partnerships with educational institutions and community organizations that focus on diversity. Additionally, mentoring programs can provide guidance and support to individuals from various backgrounds, helping them to navigate their careers in cybersecurity. Training sessions that focus on unconscious bias can also contribute to a more inclusive workplace by creating awareness and encouraging employees to confront their biases. As organizations work towards a more inclusive environment, they will not only attract a wider talent pool but also foster a sense of belonging that can drive employee engagement and retention.

Moving forward, it's imperative for cybersecurity professionals to recognize their role in fostering a more diverse workforce. Engaging in advocacy, supporting initiatives that aim to empower underrepresented groups, and actively participating in discussions about diversity can create a ripple effect that influences the entire industry. Networking events focused on diversity can connect professionals across various backgrounds, creating opportunities for knowledge sharing and collaboration. The future will belong to those organizations that not only recognize the potential of diverse teams but actively work to cultivate them. As you consider your role in this space, remember that every effort towards inclusion not only benefits your organization but also strengthens the cybersecurity field as a whole.

5. Regulatory Landscape and Compliance Trends

5.1 GDPR Evolution and Its Global Impact

The General Data Protection Regulation, commonly known as GDPR, emerged on May 25, 2018, representing a pivotal moment in the landscape of data protection legislation. Enforced by the European Union, GDPR set a high standard for how businesses handle personal data across the globe. This regulation stressed individual privacy rights and imposed strict compliance obligations on organizations that process personal information. Companies worldwide, irrespective of their location, had to adapt their data handling practices to align with these regulations to avoid significant fines. As a result, GDPR not only affected European companies but also had a ripple effect on businesses around the world, compelling them to rethink their data protection strategies, establish clear protocols for data processing, and enhance their overall cybersecurity measures.

Looking towards the future, the influence of GDPR will likely expand as data protection becomes an even more pressing concern for governments and regulatory bodies worldwide. There is a growing recognition that the challenges posed by digital data systems require a unified approach to privacy protection. Countries outside the EU are beginning to draft their regulations inspired by GDPR, seen in regions such as Asia and South America, where local governments are increasingly enacting laws that emphasize similar data privacy rights and compliance frameworks. As we approach 2025, organizations will need to keep a close watch on how GDPR evolves, especially regarding enforcement mechanisms and potential amendments. This ongoing transformation will shape not only corporate governance on data privacy but also the overall global standard for protecting sensitive information, driving businesses toward enhanced transparency and accountability in their data management practices.

Cybersecurity professionals should prioritize an understanding of GDPR's implications, recognizing that adapting to the evolving landscape of data protection laws is crucial. While navigating these regulations, establishing frameworks to enhance data privacy and compliance will not only mitigate risks but also build trust with clients and consumers. Staying informed about international trends and preparing for potential legal changes will empower organizations to maintain robust data protection practices, ensuring they remain ahead in an increasingly complex environment.

5.2 Emerging Regulations: What to Expect in 2025

As we look towards 2025, the landscape of cybersecurity regulations is becoming increasingly complex and multifaceted. Governments and regulatory bodies around the world are recognizing the critical need for robust cybersecurity measures to protect against rising threats. Upcoming legislation is expected to establish stricter guidelines for data privacy, incident reporting, and breach notification processes. For instance, countries may implement comprehensive frameworks similar to the European Union's GDPR, emphasizing transparency, accountability, and user consent. These regulations will likely compel organizations to adopt more stringent cybersecurity practices, influencing everything from how data is collected and stored to how security incidents are managed and disclosed. The anticipated laws will not only set the baseline for security compliance but also serve as a catalyst for innovation in cybersecurity technologies.

Organizations must begin preparing for these forthcoming regulatory changes to avoid non-compliance penalties and potential reputational damage. A proactive approach involves conducting thorough assessments of current cybersecurity policies and practices, aligning them with projected regulatory requirements. Companies should invest in regular training programs for employees to ensure they understand the significance of compliance and the role they play in maintaining security. Additionally, adopting a risk management framework can help organizations identify vulnerabilities and address them ahead of time. Collaboration with legal experts and cybersecurity professionals will be crucial to stay informed about evolving regulations and to develop strategies that not only meet compliance standards but also enhance overall security posture. Establishing strong communication channels with stakeholders will further enable companies to pivot quickly as new legal landscapes emerge.

Staying ahead requires vigilance and adaptability. As regulatory expectations evolve, actively participating in industry forums and engaging with regulators can provide valuable insights into emerging trends and compliance challenges. By embedding regulatory considerations into their cybersecurity strategies early on, organizations can cultivate a culture of security that thrives amid change. This preparedness not only mitigates risks but also positions them advantageously in an increasingly competitive market, where consumers are more aware and concerned about data privacy than ever before.

5.3 The Role of Compliance in Cybersecurity Strategy

Organizations today face an ever-evolving landscape of cyber threats, making it essential to build a solid compliance framework. Adopting frameworks such as ISO 27001, the NIST Cybersecurity Framework, and GDPR not only helps in adhering to legal requirements but establishes trust with customers and stakeholders. These frameworks provide structured guidelines that define how organizations can protect sensitive information, manage risks, and respond to incidents effectively. The key to selecting a suitable framework lies in understanding the specific needs of the organization and the regulatory landscape within which it operates. As we look ahead to 2025, expect these frameworks to adapt, with increased focus on automation and integration with advanced technologies such as artificial intelligence and machine learning to enhance compliance monitoring and reporting.

Moreover, with the rise of cloud computing and remote work arrangements, compliance frameworks are likely to incorporate more extensive provisions for third-party risks and data privacy. Organizations will need to ensure that their partners comply with their standards, thereby creating a more comprehensive compliance network that extends beyond their internal practices. This approach will foster a culture of compliance throughout the supply chain, enhancing overall cybersecurity posture in the process.

Seamlessly integrating compliance into broader cybersecurity strategies is crucial for 2025 and beyond. Organizations should view compliance not as a separate entity but as an integral part of their security operations. This means aligning compliance efforts with risk management and cybersecurity initiatives so that they reinforce each other. A successful integration strategy involves establishing clear lines of communication between compliance officers, IT security teams, and executive management. Techniques like cross-functional training and regular joint meetings can help maintain this alignment.

As cybersecurity threats become more sophisticated, organizations will benefit from adopting a risk-based approach to compliance. By prioritizing compliance activities based on the organization's unique risk profile, resources can be allocated more effectively, ensuring critical vulnerabilities are addressed first. Additionally, the use of advanced analytics and dashboard reporting can provide real-time insights into compliance status, allowing organizations to make informed decisions quickly. This proactive stance not only enhances compliance but provides a strategic advantage against potential cyber threats.

Staying informed about the latest compliance trends and technology advancements will be advantageous. Regularly reviewing and updating policies, leveraging automated compliance tools, and conducting simulated audits can help organizations navigate the complex landscape of cybersecurity compliance efficiently.

6. Internet of Things (IoT) Security Challenges

6.1 Securing a Broader IoT Ecosystem

The Internet of Things (IoT) has revolutionized how devices communicate, enhancing efficiency and enabling new applications across various sectors. However, the rapid expansion of this landscape comes with significant vulnerabilities that cyber security professionals must address. These vulnerabilities range from insecure communication protocols, weak authentication methods, and inadequate data protection measures, to issues stemming from legacy systems that have not kept pace with evolving threats. Devices lacking robust security features can be easily exploited, leading to unauthorized access and data breaches. Understanding these vulnerabilities requires a holistic perspective, analyzing not only the individual devices but also the networks on which they operate and the broader ecosystem of interconnected systems. By identifying potential weak points, professionals can create a detailed risk assessment and prioritize areas that need immediate attention.

To effectively secure the IoT ecosystem, adopting a holistic security approach is crucial. This involves frameworks that encompass all components, from end-user devices to backend systems and cloud services. Implementing risk management frameworks such as the NIST Cybersecurity Framework can guide professionals in establishing a robust security posture. Furthermore, embracing security by design ensures that security considerations are integrated into the development lifecycle of IoT devices. Regular software updates and patch management are essential practices to mitigate vulnerabilities over time. In addition, a layered security strategy that combines endpoint protection, network security, and strong encryption methods provides a comprehensive defense against potential attacks. It is also invaluable to engage all stakeholders, including device manufacturers, service providers, and end-users, to foster a shared responsibility for security within the IoT ecosystem.

Cyber security professionals looking forward to 2025 must also be prepared for evolving trends in IoT security. As artificial intelligence and machine learning become more prevalent, these technologies can be leveraged to predict and respond to security incidents in real time. Additionally, the rise of edge computing will necessitate new security paradigms, as data processing occurs closer to where it is generated. Understanding these trends will empower professionals to devise proactive strategies that anticipate future challenges. It's beneficial to cultivate a mindset of continuous improvement, staying abreast of emerging threats and technologies while fostering a culture of security awareness across all levels of the organization. A practical tip is to conduct regular security training sessions, helping stakeholders recognize potential threats and affirming the importance of security in their everyday practices. Engagement and education will serve as a foundation for building a secure IoT ecosystem.

6.2 Innovations in Device Authentication

Authentication techniques have evolved significantly in recent years, particularly in the realm of Internet of Things (IoT) devices. As these devices proliferate, traditional password-based systems become increasingly inadequate due to their vulnerability and the sheer number of devices that require secure access. New methods such as biometrics, which recognize unique physical characteristics like fingerprints or facial patterns, are becoming more mainstream. Similarly, behavioural biometrics is gaining traction, analyzing user patterns like typing speed or mouse movements to identify users based on their typical behaviour rather than static credentials. Additionally, the use of blockchain technology offers a decentralized approach to device authentication, making it harder for unauthorized entities to forge identities. This not only enhances security but also streamlines the process, providing a more seamless user experience. Innovations like federated authentication, where multiple systems share authentication responsibilities, are also key trends, especially in environments where devices from different manufacturers need to communicate securely.

While these innovations are promising, they also introduce a set of challenges that cybersecurity professionals must address. One major issue is the complexity of managing diverse authentication methods across an array of devices, which increases the risk of misconfigurations. Additionally, many new authentication methods still have maturity and reliability issues, especially in terms of user adoption and resistance to change. These challenges necessitate robust solutions, such as developing standard protocols that all devices must follow, ensuring consistency in security measures across manufacturers. Moreover, integrating artificial intelligence can help automate threat detection in authentication systems, flagging anomalies that suggest compromised devices or user accounts. Cybersecurity education and awareness are also crucial as users must be informed about the proper use and limitations of these authentication methods to avoid common pitfalls.

In this rapidly evolving landscape, staying informed about the latest advancements and emerging threats is essential for cybersecurity professionals. Understanding the nuances of these innovations enables better strategies to enhance the security of device authentication. Fostering an environment that encourages technological advancements while implementing holistic security measures will be crucial as we look ahead. A practical tip for professionals is to continuously evaluate the efficacy of current authentication methods and remain open to adopting new technologies that can lead to more secure authentication practices.

6.3 Addressing the Security Flaws in Consumer Electronics

Consumer electronics face numerous security risks that have become more pronounced as devices become smarter and more interconnected. From smart TVs capturing personal data to wearable fitness trackers susceptible to hacking, the vulnerabilities in these devices pose significant risks to consumer privacy and security. IoT devices, which are increasingly integrated into homes, create additional entry points for cybercriminals, often utilizing outdated software or lacking adequate security measures. Many consumers are unaware that their devices continually collect data, and without proper safeguards, this information can be accessed by malicious actors. The widespread adoption of these technologies has outpaced the implementation of robust security protocols, leading to an environment where data breaches and unauthorized access are prevalent concerns for both users and manufacturers.

To combat these security flaws, manufacturers must prioritize the integration of robust security features within their devices from the design phase. This includes implementing end-to-end encryption for data transmission and ensuring that software updates are pushed promptly to address newly discovered vulnerabilities. Manufacturers should also adopt a security-by-design philosophy, incorporating security measures such as secure booting and intrusion detection systems. For consumers, the first line of defense is awareness. Being informed about the privacy policies of devices, understanding the implications of data sharing, and regularly updating device firmware can significantly reduce risks. Additionally, utilizing unique passwords and enabling two-factor authentication wherever possible adds an extra layer of security. Manufacturers and consumers must collaboratively take responsibility for security; manufacturers must build safer products, while consumers must use them wisely.

As we move further into 2025, staying informed about potential security risks and advancements in protective measures is crucial. Embracing a proactive approach toward cybersecurity will also involve continuous education for both manufacturers and consumers on the latest threats and prevention techniques. By fostering a culture of security mindfulness, where both parties are invested in safeguarding data and respecting privacy, we can create a safer environment for the growing ecosystem of consumer electronics. It is essential to regularly audit and assess security measures in use, ensuring ongoing vigilance against evolving threats. Utilizing comprehensive security solutions and maintaining clear communication about risks can significantly mitigate the challenges posed by the rapidly changing landscape of consumer technology.

7. Cybersecurity in the Age of Quantum Computing

7.1 Understanding Quantum Threats to Cryptography

Quantum computing represents a significant shift in the way we process information. Unlike traditional computers that use bits as the smallest unit of data, quantum computers utilize quantum bits, or qubits. Qubits can exist in multiple states simultaneously due to the principles of superposition and entanglement. This property allows quantum computers to perform complex calculations at speeds that are impossible for classical computers. The implications for cybersecurity are profound. Traditional cryptographic systems rely on mathematical problems that are computationally hard for classical computers to solve, such as factoring large prime numbers. However, with the advent of quantum computing, these problems may no longer be secure. Quantum algorithms, such as Shor's algorithm, have the potential to break widely used encryption systems, making the understanding of quantum mechanics not just an academic exercise, but a crucial aspect of modern cybersecurity.

The threat landscape of cybersecurity is changing, and quantum computing is at the forefront of this transformation. Traditional cryptographic methods, including RSA and ECC (Elliptic Curve Cryptography), have served as the backbone of secure communications for decades. However, these systems rely on the difficulty of mathematical problems that quantum computers can easily solve. As quantum computing technology advances, the vulnerability of these cryptographic systems grows. It is estimated that a sufficiently powerful quantum computer could break RSA encryption in a matter of seconds. This poses a significant risk to sensitive data and communications worldwide. Organizations that rely on encryption for data protection must begin to reassess their security strategies. Quantum-resistant algorithms are being developed as a response, but the transition to these new standards requires both time and careful planning. Transitioning to post-quantum cryptographic methods is not merely a technical challenge but also a strategic necessity to safeguard data in an increasingly quantum-capable future.

As we look towards 2025, it is essential for cybersecurity professionals to stay informed about the evolution of quantum computing. Regularly assessing the vulnerability of existing systems to quantum threats and investing in education around quantum-resistant technologies will be crucial. Engaging in discussions about quantum security strategies within your organization can enhance preparedness. Monitoring developments in quantum computing research and potential shifts in government regulations concerning quantum threats will also aid in adapting security measures appropriately. By proactively addressing these challenges, cybersecurity professionals can better protect sensitive data against the impending quantum threat.

7.2 Preparing for Quantum-Resistant Algorithms

The emergence of quantum-resistant algorithms is a significant development in the field of cryptography, especially as we approach an era where quantum computers could compromise traditional encryption methods. As quantum technology advances, the potential for these machines to break widely used cryptographic systems highlights the urgency of transitioning to quantum-resistant alternatives. These new algorithms are designed to secure data against attacks from quantum algorithms like Shor's Algorithm, which can efficiently factor large integers and compute discrete logarithms, allowing access to sensitive information that was previously secure. Efforts are currently underway, spearheaded by organizations such as NIST, to establish standards for post-quantum cryptography, focusing on lattice-based, hash-based, code-based, and multivariate polynomial cryptography, among others. It's not just about replacing old algorithms; it's about rethinking how we understand security in a world where quantum computing can change the landscape drastically.

However, implementing these new quantum-resistant algorithms is fraught with challenges that organizations must navigate. The shift to post-quantum cryptography is not a simple plug-and-play solution; it requires holistic changes to systems and processes. One of the primary challenges is operational complexity. Many organizations have established extensive cryptographic infrastructures, and integrating new algorithms requires thorough testing and validation to avoid introducing vulnerabilities. There's also the difficulty of ensuring compatibility with existing systems. Legacy systems may not be easily adaptable, leading to the potential need for expensive updates or replacements. Additionally, training staff to understand and effectively employ these new algorithms is critical; without proper knowledge, the risk of misconfiguration rises significantly. Security professionals must also grapple with the uncertain landscape of quantum computing advancements, making it challenging to predict the timelines and directions of both quantum capabilities and the corresponding defenses. Navigating these complexities requires a strategic approach that accounts for both immediate needs and future scalability.

As organizations prepare for the quantum computing revolution, prioritizing a proactive stance towards quantum-resistant algorithms is essential. Succinctly, it involves conducting thorough risk assessments that consider the specific threats posed by quantum capabilities. Staying informed on the latest developments in quantum technology and cryptography will be crucial. Organizations should also engage in developing a roadmap that includes milestones for testing and implementing chosen quantum-resistant algorithms. Collaborating with cryptographic experts and participating in industry forums can provide valuable insights and aid in creating robust security frameworks. Ultimately, adopting a forward-thinking approach not only enhances security but also positions organizations advantageously in the fast-evolving cyber landscape of the future.

7.3 The Future of Cryptographic Frameworks

The evolution of cryptographic frameworks is shaped largely by the impending reality of quantum computing. As we look toward 2025, it's essential to understand the implications of quantum advancements on current security practices. Traditional encryption methods, such as RSA and ECC, rely on the computational difficulty of specific mathematical problems, which quantum computers threaten to solve efficiently. Researchers and practitioners in the field are actively developing quantum-resistant algorithms as a proactive response to this looming threat. These new frameworks not only incorporate post-quantum cryptography standards but also blend classical methodologies with innovative techniques. This hybrid approach will be crucial in creating layers of security that can withstand both classical and quantum attacks, ensuring that sensitive data remains protected in an uncertain technological landscape.

Organizations must stay ahead of quantum threats by adopting strategic measures that prioritize both awareness and innovation. This involves investing in research and development to explore and implement quantum-resistant cryptographic algorithms. Integrating flexible security policies that allow for rapid updates to cryptographic practices will also be vital as standards evolve. Furthermore, cybersecurity professionals should foster collaboration across sectors, sharing knowledge and solutions to accelerate the adoption of resilient frameworks. Training personnel on the implications of quantum computing and promoting a culture of security awareness can empower teams to adapt more readily. Those who take a proactive stance, pilot new technologies, and engage with the cybersecurity community will undoubtedly lead the charge in safeguarding information against quantum vulnerabilities.

As we navigate the complexities of quantum computing, it's critical to remain informed and flexible in our approaches to cryptography. Keeping abreast of ongoing developments in both quantum research and cryptographic algorithm design will serve organizations well. Regularly updated risk assessments will help gauge potential vulnerabilities, allowing organizations to pivot strategies as needed. Keeping communication lines open with industry peers can unveil emerging threats and solutions from diverse perspectives, enhancing collective resilience. Finally, investing in educational initiatives can ensure that teams are equipped with the latest knowledge to defend against tomorrow's challenges.

8. Privacy Enhancements and Personal Data Protection

8.1 Evolving Privacy Regulations and Their Implications

The current privacy landscape is characterized by a patchwork of regulations that vary widely across regions and sectors. While the General Data Protection Regulation (GDPR) in Europe has set a high standard for data protection and privacy rights, numerous other regulations have emerged in different jurisdictions. In the United States, for example, the California Consumer Privacy Act (CCPA) has unveiled significant requirements for data handling practices, emphasizing transparency and consumer control over personal data. Organizations are now navigating a complex array of requirements that stem not only from GDPR and CCPA but also from sector-specific laws like HIPAA for healthcare and COPPA for children's online privacy. This regulatory environment has compelled businesses to invest heavily in compliance strategies, reshaping how they collect, store, and process data. In an era where breaches can lead to severe penalties and reputational damage, understanding these regulations is paramount for cybersecurity professionals tasked with safeguarding sensitive information.

Looking towards the future, the landscape of privacy regulations is expected to evolve further, possibly leading to more unified frameworks that streamline compliance efforts across borders. The potential for federal privacy legislation in the U.S. looms large, which could harmonize a variety of state-level regulations into a singular set of requirements. Additionally, as technology advances, we may witness the introduction of regulations that specifically address emerging technologies such as artificial intelligence and the Internet of Things. Cybersecurity professionals need to stay ahead by actively engaging with legal experts and advocacy groups, anticipating changes, and evaluating current policies to ensure their organizations are prepared to meet new obligations as they arise. The rise of public interest in data privacy will likely push lawmakers to adopt stricter policies, therefore, continuous monitoring of legislative trends and active participation in compliance discussions will be critical in navigating this evolving regulatory landscape.

To effectively prepare for the future of privacy regulations, organizations should adopt a proactive approach. This involves not only understanding existing laws but also fostering a culture of privacy that permeates every level of the organization. Implementing robust data governance frameworks, conducting regular audits, and prioritizing transparency can enhance an organization's compliance posture. Training employees on privacy best practices and integrating privacy by design principles into product development can create a resilient defense against regulatory changes. As the demand for data privacy evolves, staying informed and adaptable will not just help organizations comply but also build trust with consumers who are increasingly concerned about how their information is handled.

8.2 Technologies Enhancing User Privacy

Privacy-enhancing technologies are evolving rapidly and play a crucial role in safeguarding users' digital identities. In 2025, innovations such as advanced encryption methods, homomorphic encryption, and zero-knowledge proofs are becoming more accessible and widely implemented. These technologies enable data to be processed and analyzed without revealing the underlying information, thus maintaining user privacy while leveraging data's analytical power. Moreover, decentralized identity systems help eliminate the reliance on centralized databases, allowing users to control their personal data and share only what is necessary. Biometric security measures, enhanced through AI and machine learning, can further bolster privacy by providing a secure means of access without the need for traditional passwords. As these technologies develop, organizations can integrate user privacy into their core functions, ensuring that privacy becomes a fundamental aspect of user interaction with digital platforms.

The challenge lies in harmonizing these privacy technologies with the overarching business objectives. Companies are discovering that prioritizing user privacy can align with their strategic goals, particularly in fostering trust among consumers and enhancing brand loyalty. However, integrating privacy-enhancing technologies requires a nuanced understanding of both technical capabilities and business imperatives. Organizations must explore ways to incorporate these technologies without compromising operational efficiency or profit margins. This could involve adopting privacy by design principles, where privacy considerations are embedded into the product development lifecycle, or leveraging transparent data processes to build trust with consumers. Striking this balance not only enhances user privacy but also positions businesses favourably in a market increasingly driven by consumer awareness around data protection.

In the coming years, cyber security professionals must stay ahead of the curve by understanding these emerging technologies and their implications. Engaging with privacy-enhancing technologies requires continuous learning and adaptation, as both privacy regulations and consumer expectations evolve. Regularly collaborating with cross-functional teams, including legal and marketing departments, can ensure that privacy initiatives align with business goals and regulatory compliance. Professionals should also advocate for greater investment in these technologies, as the costs of data breaches and privacy failures can far exceed the investments in preventative solutions. Keeping abreast of technology trends and maintaining a proactive stance on privacy will not only protect users but also create an environment where businesses can thrive amidst increasing scrutiny over privacy practices.

8.3 Balancing Privacy with Business Objectives

The conflict between privacy and profit has become increasingly prominent as businesses navigate a landscape filled with evolving technology and shifting consumer expectations. In the digital age, data has emerged as a central asset for organizations, enabling them to enhance customer experiences, target marketing efforts, and drive profitability. However, this growing dependence on data comes with heightened scrutiny regarding privacy. Consumers are becoming more aware of their digital footprint and demand greater transparency on how their information is handled. This tension creates a significant challenge for businesses as they strive to maintain trust while also maximizing their bottom line. Companies that prioritize aggressive data collection and underplay privacy concerns may face backlash, damaging their reputation and losing customer loyalty. Conversely, those that adopt stringent privacy measures without considering the business implications may miss out on valuable insights that could drive growth.

Crafting a balanced approach between privacy and profitability requires innovative thinking and a commitment to ethical practices. Organizations must begin by integrating privacy into their business strategies from the ground up. This means embracing privacy as a core value rather than a compliance obligation. Employing privacy by design principles can help businesses create systems and processes that inherently respect user data. By actively engaging with customers and clearly communicating data practices, companies can cultivate trust that translates into customer loyalty. Another key strategy is leveraging technology that enhances data security while allowing for data-driven insights. Advanced analytics tools can provide valuable information without compromising user privacy, thus allowing businesses to maintain competitive advantage while honouring consumer expectations. Investing in staff training on data ethics can further help foster a culture of responsibility toward privacy, ensuring that every employee understands the importance of safeguarding customer information. Companies that adopt this balanced approach position themselves not just for compliance but for sustainable success in an increasingly privacy-conscious marketplace. A practical tip for organizations is to regularly review and update their privacy policies, engaging customers in the process to enhance transparency and build confidence in their brand.

9. Cybersecurity Culture and Awareness

9.1 Building a Cyber-Aware Organization

Creating a culture of security within an organization is crucial for ensuring that cybersecurity is not merely seen as the responsibility of the IT department, but as a shared value upheld by everyone. As threats evolve and become more sophisticated, fostering a security-centric culture helps ensure that employees understand their roles in protecting sensitive information. Training programs can no longer be one-time events; instead, they should be ongoing dialogues that actively involve all staff. Regular discussions about risks, the latest threat intelligence, and real-world case studies can reinforce the significance of cyber awareness across all levels of the organization.

A security-centric culture thrives on transparency and open communication. Encouraging employees to report suspicious activities without fear of repercussion promotes an environment of trust. This helps not only in identifying potential threats but also in building a collective consciousness about cybersecurity. Integrating security topics into regular meetings and organizational updates can ensure that the focus remains strong. Employees feel empowered when they recognize their part in safeguarding organizational assets, making them more likely to adhere to security protocols and stay informed about best practices.

To cultivate cyber awareness among employees, organizations must implement comprehensive training programs tailored to various job functions and risk levels. One effective strategy is gamification, where security concepts are woven into engaging formats such as quizzes or simulated phishing attacks. This not only captures employees' interest but also reinforces learning by providing them with practical, hands-on experience. Additionally, creating bite-sized content that can be consumed quickly allows for continuous learning, fitting conveniently into busy work schedules.

Regular assessments and feedback loops are essential to measure the effectiveness of training initiatives. By soliciting input from employees about their understanding of cybersecurity best practices and perceived effectiveness of training sessions, organizations can adapt their strategies as needed. It is also vital to celebrate successes and acknowledge individuals or teams who exemplify strong cyber hygiene. This recognition reinforces the importance of collective responsibility and motivates others to enhance their own cybersecurity practices. One practical tip is to establish a monthly security theme that focuses on different aspects of cybersecurity, which can keep the conversation relevant and engaging while helping to maintain a high level of awareness throughout the organization.

9.2 The Role of Training Simulations

Training simulations offer a unique way to enhance employee preparedness in the rapidly evolving field of cybersecurity. These simulations provide numerous advantages, allowing professionals to engage with real-world scenarios without the risks associated with actual attacks. One of the key benefits is increased retention of knowledge. Employees who experience situations firsthand are more likely to remember protocols and responses when a real incident occurs. Additionally, simulations allow for the immediate application of theoretical knowledge, reinforcing learning through practical experience. Such immersive training builds confidence, as participants learn to navigate crisis situations, make decisions under pressure, and understand the consequences of their actions. Another advantage is the ability to assess and improve problem-solving skills. By simulating various attack vectors, organizations can observe how employees respond and where their strengths and weaknesses lie, allowing for targeted training that addresses specific gaps in knowledge or skills.

Designing effective training simulations requires careful consideration of several key elements. First, the simulation must be realistic and relevant to the specific threats that cyber professionals face. This means involving subject matter experts to ensure the scenarios reflect current trends and tactics used by cyber adversaries. It's also essential to incorporate diverse situations, including both common and advanced attack strategies. Furthermore, a well-structured simulation includes comprehensive feedback mechanisms. Participants should receive constructive feedback on their performance, which can enhance their understanding and lead to improvement.

Incorporating a debriefing session afterward is crucial, as it allows participants to reflect on their actions and decisions, discussing what was successful and what could be improved. Technological tools such as virtual environments and gamification can also enhance engagement and offer a more dynamic learning experience.

To maximize the effectiveness of training simulations, organizations should consider integrating them into a broader training and development strategy. This means establishing a continuous cycle of training, practice, and assessment that evolves alongside the threat landscape. Regularly updating simulation scenarios to reflect new vulnerabilities and attack methods ensures that cybersecurity professionals remain prepared for emerging challenges. Moreover, fostering a culture that encourages learning from mistakes can significantly enhance the value of simulations. Employees should feel comfortable exploring different approaches and experimenting during training sessions, as this can lead to innovative solutions and a more resilient cybersecurity posture.

9.3 Measuring the Effectiveness of Awareness Programs

Measuring the effectiveness of cybersecurity awareness programs is crucial for ensuring that organizations can defend against evolving threats. Metrics and Key Performance Indicators (KPIs) should be established to evaluate success. Key metrics include participation rates, retention of knowledge, and the reduction of security incidents attributed to human error. Organizations can leverage pre- and post-training assessments to quantify knowledge gain and behavioural changes among employees. Tracking the number of reported phishing attempts and incidents stemming from insider actions can provide a clear picture of the program's impact. Additionally, engagement levels can be analyzed through follow-up surveys and feedback forms, which can reveal how well employees are internalizing the concepts taught. Another vital metric to consider is the frequency of security-related inquiries from employees, as an increase may indicate that staff feel more empowered to ask questions and seek clarification on security protocols.

Continuous improvement is essential in adapting to the fast-paced world of cybersecurity. As threats continue to evolve, so should the awareness programs. One strategy to enhance effectiveness is to regularly update training content to reflect the latest threats, techniques, and technologies. Involving employees in the design of the program can create a more engaging experience, ensuring that the learning material resonates with them. Conducting frequent review sessions and live simulation exercises can solidify knowledge and improve the likelihood of employees responding appropriately in real situations. Utilizing data analytics to understand common pain points can also guide future training and make it more relevant. Importantly, fostering a culture of security within the organization encourages continuous dialogue about safe online behaviours and reinforces the importance of vigilance at all times.

Giving employees the chance to share their experiences and challenges in dealing with real-world threats can significantly enhance awareness efforts. Consider arranging workshops or informal meetups where staff can discuss security scenarios. This interactive approach not only shares knowledge but also builds a more coherent security-focused community within the organization, making everyone feel responsible for contributing to the overall security posture. In moving towards 2025, staying agile and responsive to changes in the cybersecurity landscape will ensure that awareness programs not only meet current demands but also pave the way for a more resilient future.

10. Incident Response and Recovery Trends

10.1 Developing a Comprehensive Incident Response Plan

An effective incident response plan is critical for any organization aiming to protect its digital assets and maintain operational integrity in the face of cyber threats. At its core, the incident response plan should include defined roles and responsibilities to ensure that everyone knows their part during an incident. This clarity helps streamline the response process, reducing confusion under pressure. Another essential component is a clear communication strategy, which ensures accurate and timely information is relayed both internally and externally. This is particularly important when incidents escalate, as stakeholders will look for reassurances and updates. Additionally, establishing a robust incident detection and analysis process allows teams to categorize incidents accurately and prioritize their responses based on the severity and potential impact. Furthermore, the incorporation of forensic tools and analytics can enhance the understanding of the attack vectors and methods used by cybercriminals, leading to better pre-emptive measures in the future.

Testing and refining incident response plans is vital to ensure they remain effective amid evolving threats. One of the best practices is conducting regular tabletop exercises that simulate various incident scenarios. These exercises provide an opportunity for team members to practice their responses in a controlled environment, identify weaknesses in the plan, and build confidence in their roles. Another effective method is real-time simulations or red team-blue team exercises, where one group actively attempts to breach security measures while the other works to defend against the attack. This dynamic offers insights into the effectiveness of the incident response strategy and team readiness. Additionally, after any incident, a thorough post-incident review should occur. This review should analyze what occurred, how the team responded, and what could be improved. It's essential to incorporate lessons learned into the incident response plan, fostering a continuous improvement culture that prioritizes resilience. Engaging in intelligence sharing with other organizations or industry groups can also provide valuable insights, ensuring your response plans evolve alongside the threat landscape.

Regularly updating incident response plans to reflect changes in the organization, technology, or threat landscape is a practical tip that should not be overlooked. Keeping this documentation current is just as important as the preparation itself, ensuring that when a real incident occurs, every team member is well-prepared and the organization is equipped to respond effectively.

10.2 The Importance of Post-Incident Analysis

Post-incident analysis is an essential component of any cybersecurity strategy because it allows organizations to learn from previous attacks and bolster their defenses. In an increasingly complex digital landscape, understanding the motivations and methods of cybercriminals is crucial for anticipating future threats. Each incident provides an opportunity to analyze vulnerabilities in systems, processes, and personnel. By thoroughly examining incidents and their consequences, organizations can identify weak spots and inform their security protocols, ultimately leading to stronger defense mechanisms. As we move towards 2025, the importance of this continuous loop of learning becomes even more apparent, since cyber threats are evolving at an unprecedented pace. Organizations that invest time and resources into post-incident analysis not only protect themselves from future breaches but also enhance their overall cybersecurity posture.

Furthermore, engaging in post-incident analysis creates a culture of accountability and vigilance within teams. When cybersecurity professionals are encouraged to reflect on what happened during incidents, they are more likely to take proactive measures rather than merely reacting to threats as they arise. This proactive approach promotes a mindset geared towards constant improvement and adaptation, which is vital as we anticipate the coming trends in cybersecurity—like artificial intelligence and machine learning being weaponized by both sides in the cyber battleground. The insights gained from past incidents become foundational for future training and awareness programs, equipping personnel with knowledge that improves overall organizational resilience against attack vectors.

Turning data into actionable insights is one of the key challenges that organizations face after an incident. It's not enough to merely document what has happened; cybersecurity teams must distil the critical lessons from an incident that can inform better practices and strategies going forward. One effective method is to conduct a lessons learned session shortly after an incident, where team members can openly discuss what transpired, what worked, what didn't, and how improvements can be made. This collaborative approach fosters creativity and ensures that diverse perspectives are taken into account, ideally resulting in more comprehensive insights.

Additionally, leveraging technology tools can significantly enhance the process of deriving actionable insights. Using data analytics and visualization tools enables teams to sift through large volumes of incident data and identify patterns and anomalous behaviour more efficiently. By applying machine learning algorithms to past incidents, organizations can not only speed up incident response times but also make predictions about potential future attacks. These strategies will empower cybersecurity professionals to formulate robust incident response plans that are both adaptive and informed by real-world data.

As organizations prepare for the evolving threat landscape of 2025, the ability to create actionable insights will set them apart in their resilience against cyberattacks. Investing in continuous improvement and effective data utilization can transform a reactive post-incident analysis process into a proactive strategy that not only addresses vulnerabilities but also strengthens overall security infrastructure. Remember, the ultimate goal is to empower teams to anticipate issues before they escalate into incidents.

10.3 Leveraging Automation in Incident Management

Automation is revolutionizing how cybersecurity professionals handle incident management, drastically shortening response times and improving the overall effectiveness of security measures. In the face of increasing threats and complexities in the digital landscape, automation allows teams to respond to incidents with unprecedented speed and efficiency. When an incident occurs, automation can initiate predefined workflows that trigger alerts, gather relevant data, and notify the appropriate stakeholders without the need for manual intervention. This immediate response not only mitigates potential damage but also enables teams to focus on strategic decision-making rather than on repetitive tasks.

Moreover, the integration of machine learning and artificial intelligence into automation tools enhances their capability to analyze patterns within data, which aids in recognizing anomalies that may indicate a security breach. By leveraging automation for monitoring and analysis, cybersecurity professionals can proactively identify and address vulnerabilities before they escalate into incidents. The fusion of automation with incident response leads to a more dynamic way of managing security threats, equipping teams with the agility to adapt to ever-evolving cyber threats.

Choosing the right automation tools is critical to the success of incident management efforts. Security orchestration, automation, and response (SOAR) platforms are emerging as key solutions for enhancing incident response capabilities. These platforms provide a centralized way to manage security tools, allowing for seamless integration of various technologies like Security Information and Event Management (SIEM) systems, threat intelligence platforms, and endpoint detection tools. The ability to harmonize these tools results in more coherent incident management processes that are not only quicker but also smarter, leveraging shared data for improved analytics and response strategies.

When evaluating automation tools, it is essential to consider factors such as ease of integration, scalability, and the ability to customize workflows according to specific organizational needs. Furthermore, with the rapid development in automation technologies, cybersecurity professionals should remain informed about the latest advancements and trends to ensure they are utilizing the best solutions available. A practical approach is to adopt a phased implementation strategy, allowing teams to adapt gradually to automation while continually refining processes based on feedback and performance metrics.

In this evolving landscape, keeping updated on the capabilities of automation tools will help cybersecurity professionals make informed decisions that enhance their incident management frameworks and bolster their overall security posture.

11. Emerging Technologies and Their Security Implications

11.1 Blockchain and Cybersecurity Applications

Blockchain technology fundamentally transforms how we think about security. At its core, a blockchain is a decentralized ledger that records transactions across many computers so that the record cannot be altered retroactively. This immutability is crucial in cybersecurity, where data integrity is paramount. In a world where cyber threats are becoming increasingly sophisticated, the transparent and tamper-resistant nature of blockchain presents a compelling advantage. It offers an additional layer of security against data breaches and unauthorized access by ensuring that every transaction is validated by multiple parties before being added to the chain. Moreover, blockchain can enhance identity management, allowing users to control their digital identities and reduce the risk of identity theft. By utilizing cryptographic techniques, blockchain can provide a more secure channel for transmitting sensitive information, thus lowering the chances of interception by malicious actors.

Several companies and organizations have begun to implement blockchain solutions to bolster their cybersecurity measures. For instance, a notable case is that of a major financial institution that adopted blockchain to secure its internal communications and transaction processes. By integrating blockchain, the institution was able to create a secure environment where all transaction records were immutable and verifiable in real-time. This led to a significant reduction in fraud cases as security incidents could be traced back to their origins more efficiently. Another example can be found in supply chain management, where a multinational company leveraged blockchain to enhance the authenticity of its product tracking system. By recording every step of the supply chain on a blockchain, the company not only ensured product integrity but also increased transparency, making it nearly impossible for counterfeit goods to enter the market. These case studies exemplify how blockchain can serve as a powerful tool in the arsenal of cybersecurity professionals.

As we look toward 2025, combining blockchain with existing cybersecurity practices can further bolster our defenses against evolving threats. Cybersecurity professionals should consider integrating blockchain technologies within their framework to enhance data privacy, improve incident response times, and streamline compliance with regulatory requirements. Fostering collaborations between blockchain developers and cybersecurity experts will be crucial in exploring innovative solutions that emerge from these intersecting domains. Keeping abreast of developments in both fields will empower professionals to leverage new tools effectively, turning potential vulnerabilities into fortified defense mechanisms. Exploring further into how smart contracts can automate and safeguard security protocols is also a practical step forward. The future of cybersecurity lies in the ability to adapt and innovate continuously, making the integration of blockchain not just advisable but essential for forward-thinking security strategies.

11.2 The Role of 5G in Cyber Threats

5G technology has rapidly transformed the telecommunications landscape, offering faster speeds, lower latency, and greater connectivity than its predecessors. This immense capability, however, brings along significant cybersecurity vulnerabilities. As 5G networks enable an unprecedented number of devices to connect simultaneously, the attack surface for potential cyber threats expands dramatically. The architecture of 5G relies on cloud-based infrastructure and a more flexible network design, which can introduce new weaknesses if not adequately secured. Moreover, the increased reliance on Internet of Things (IoT) devices under 5G can result in a multitude of entry points for cybercriminals. With devices ranging from smart appliances to critical infrastructure components interconnected, the implications of a 5G breach are profound, capable of disrupting entire systems and compromising sensitive data.

To mitigate the unique security challenges presented by 5G, organizations must adopt a multifaceted approach to cybersecurity. This includes integrating advanced encryption methods to protect data both in transit and at rest. Network slicing, a feature of 5G that allows the creation of isolated virtual networks, can be leveraged to compartmentalize services and limit exposure to threats. Implementing rigorous authentication protocols is also essential, ensuring that only authorized devices can access network resources. Regular software updates and patches on devices and infrastructure will help close vulnerabilities as they are discovered. Furthermore, fostering a culture of cybersecurity awareness among employees and end-users will empower them to recognize and respond to potential threats. Collaboration with government and industry stakeholders to establish standards and best practices for 5G security is crucial for developing a resilient cybersecurity environment.

As we look ahead to 2025, staying informed about the evolving threat landscape and the security implications of 5G will be pivotal for cybersecurity professionals. Engaging in continuous learning, attending relevant training sessions, and participating in industry forums can help build knowledge and expertise. Utilizing threat intelligence platforms will also provide valuable insights into emerging threats specific to 5G networks. By proactively addressing these issues, cybersecurity professionals can better protect assets and maintain trust in the expanding 5G ecosystem.

11.3 Security Implications of Edge Computing

Edge computing represents a shift in how data is processed, analyzed, and delivered, moving computation away from centralized data centers closer to the actual sources of data generation. This approach minimizes latency, enhances real-time processing, and optimizes bandwidth usage, making it increasingly popular in various sectors. As devices proliferate at the edge—such as IoT sensors, mobile devices, and other computing nodes—the dynamics of data management evolve. The operational implications are significant, leading to improved efficiency and speed. However, as organizations embrace edge computing to harness these benefits, they must simultaneously navigate the emerging complexities of security. Traditional cyber defense strategies may not suffice in this decentralized, distributed model, where data exits the secure confines of central servers and transits through numerous potential vulnerabilities.

Security challenges in an edge computing environment are manifold and deeply entwined with its architecture. One major concern is the increased risk of attack vectors. With data being processed at numerous edge locations, each device becomes a potential target for cyber threats. Inadequate security measures at these endpoints can lead to data breaches or unauthorized access, significantly undermining the integrity of the entire system. Furthermore, the diversity of devices and platforms involved complicates the implementation of standardized security protocols. The potential for misconfiguration, whether due to human error or oversight, can create exploitable gaps that malicious actors can exploit. As data travels over complex networks, the risk of interception and manipulation during transmission also escalates, raising concerns around data privacy and ensuring compliance with regulations such as GDPR or CCPA.

To mitigate these security challenges as we move toward 2025, professionals in cybersecurity must adopt a proactive and multifaceted approach. This includes implementing robust encryption methods for data both at rest and in transit, along with multi-factor authentication to strengthen access controls. Regular vulnerability assessments and penetration testing should become commonplace to identify and rectify weaknesses before they can be exploited. Moreover, adopting a zero-trust model, where every access request is verified regardless of its origin, can significantly bolster defenses around edge devices. Continuous monitoring and anomaly detection will also be vital to promptly identify any irregular patterns of data access or usage that could indicate a potential breach. Staying ahead means anticipating emerging threats, investing in proper training for personnel, and leveraging new technologies such as AI to enhance the overall security posture of edge computing environments.

12. Cyber Insurance and Risk Management

12.1 Understanding Cyber Insurance Policies

Cyber insurance policies are becoming essential for organizations as they navigate the complex and ever-evolving landscape of cyber threats. These policies typically cover data breaches, ransomware attacks, and various forms of cyber liability. Understanding what is included and excluded can help organizations mitigate the financial impact of an incident. However, many misconceptions persist. A common myth is that cyber insurance serves as a get out of jail free card, enabling companies to bypass the need for robust cybersecurity measures. In reality, while a comprehensive policy can provide significant financial resources to respond to an incident, it does not replace the necessity for strong cybersecurity practices. Organizations must remember that policies differ widely, with distinctions in coverage limits, deductibles, and the specific events covered, which can influence their choice of policy.

When it comes to selecting the right cyber insurance policy, organizations should consider several key criteria. First, assessing the specific risks the organization faces is crucial, as different industries may encounter unique threats. This understanding can guide companies in selecting a policy that adequately addresses their vulnerabilities. Additionally, the scope of coverage should be evaluated—policies can vary significantly in what they encompass, including legal fees, customer notification costs, data recovery, and even business interruption losses. Another important factor is the insurer's reputation and expertise in handling cyber incidents. In an age where rapid response can significantly reduce damages, having an insurer that understands the cyber landscape and offers timely support can make a difference. Organizations should also consider whether the policy requires compliance with certain security standards, as many policies today are tightening criteria to ensure the policyholder has adequate cybersecurity in place before an incident occurs. Ensuring that your organization meets these standards can lead to better outcomes during both underwriting and claims processes.

In light of 2025 trends, organizations should remain proactive by frequently reviewing and updating their cyber insurance policies. As threats evolve, so too should coverage. Regularly assessing emerging risks, changes in business operations, and the impact of new regulations will ensure an organization's policy remains relevant and effective. Furthermore, proactive engagement with insurers can reveal opportunities for enhanced coverage or better pricing. Cyber insurance is not a one-size-fits-all solution; specific needs and environments will dictate the best approach. Keeping abreast of market developments, emerging threats, and technological advancements will empower cybersecurity professionals to make informed decisions that resonate well with the organization's strategic goals.

12.2 Assessing Risk in Cybersecurity Frameworks

Risk assessment is an essential process in the ever-evolving landscape of cybersecurity. Several methodologies help organizations identify, quantify, and mitigate potential risks effectively. One prevalent technique is the FAIR (Factor Analysis of Information Risk) framework, which emphasizes quantifying risk in financial terms. This approach aids decision-makers in understanding the potential impact on their bottom line, thereby enabling more informed risk management choices. Another valuable method involves a qualitative assessment, where experts gauge risks based on their experience and judgment. This less data-heavy approach can be particularly useful for smaller organizations that may lack the resources for extensive quantitative analysis. Together, these methodologies provide a balanced view of cybersecurity risks, allowing professionals to identify vulnerabilities and make strategic decisions about which risks to address first.

Emerging technologies like machine learning and AI are becoming instrumental in risk assessment as well. These innovations can analyze vast amounts of data to identify patterns and predict potential risks based on previous incidents. Integrating these technologies into risk assessment processes not only enhances the speed and accuracy of identifying risks but also allows for real-time monitoring of systems. Additionally, scenario-based assessments help organizations envision the potential impact of various cyber threats. By simulating cyber-attack scenarios, companies can assess their readiness and the effectiveness of existing security measures. Therefore, a blend of traditional methodologies with modern technological advancements enables cybersecurity professionals to undertake comprehensive risk assessments suited for 2025 and beyond.

As organizations continue to adopt established cybersecurity frameworks like NIST, ISO/IEC 27001, and CIS Controls, integrating risk assessment into these frameworks has become increasingly important. Doing so ensures that risk management practices are not treated as standalone processes but as integral elements of a wider cybersecurity strategy. A practical approach to embedding risk assessment into these frameworks involves aligning risk management processes with the specific requirements and guidelines of the chosen framework. Organizations should establish a clear mapping between the identified risks and the framework's controls, ensuring that risk management drives security decisions across the enterprise.

Moreover, communication is vital in this integration process. Stakeholders across all levels must be engaged to foster a culture of risk awareness. Regular training and workshops can help staff understand the importance of risk assessments and how they fit into the broader context of organizational security. By integrating risk into existing frameworks, cybersecurity professionals can create a dynamic and responsive environment where risk considerations shape policy, response measures, and resource allocation. This will enable organizations to not only defend against current cyber threats but to anticipate future challenges with strategic foresight. Leveraging technology, fostering a culture of continuous improvement, and prioritizing stakeholder engagement stand out as practical steps to enhance risk integration, which will be indispensable in navigating the complexities of cybersecurity in the years ahead.

Continuously review and update your risk assessment methodologies in accordance with industry standards and evolving cyber threats. This proactive approach not only strengthens overall security but encourages a resilient and adaptable cybersecurity posture.

12.3 The Future of Risk Management Strategies

The landscape of cybersecurity is undergoing a significant transformation as organizations recognize the need for more adaptive and proactive risk management strategies. Traditional risk management methods often relied on static frameworks, which are no longer effective in addressing the dynamic nature of cyber threats. As we look toward 2025, there is a clear shift towards integrating advanced technologies such as artificial intelligence and machine learning into risk management processes. These technologies enable real-time analysis and response to emerging threats, allowing organizations to pre-emptively address vulnerabilities before they can be exploited.

Moreover, the growing importance of a holistic approach to cybersecurity is reshaping how companies view risk management. Rather than isolating cybersecurity within the IT department, organizations are beginning to foster a culture of security that involves every employee. Training and awareness programs are being implemented to ensure that all staff members understand their role in maintaining security hygiene, effectively reducing the human factor in risks. As cyber threats become more sophisticated, collaboration across departments and even industries will play a crucial role in developing resilient defense strategies that can adapt to changing landscapes.

To create risk management strategies that can withstand future challenges, there are several best practices that cybersecurity professionals should adopt. Emphasizing continuous monitoring and assessment allows organizations to recognize and respond to new threats swiftly. Implementing a risk management framework that encourages regular updates and revisions is essential, as it aligns the organization's approach with the latest cybersecurity trends and threat intelligence.

Integrating automation into risk management processes can enhance efficiency and effectiveness, as automated tools can quickly identify potential risks and suggest mitigative actions. This not only frees up valuable human resources but also enhances the organization's ability to respond to potential threats in real-time. Furthermore, fostering partnerships with cybersecurity firms and sharing information about threats can provide organizations with invaluable insights and collective defenses against cyber incidents, ultimately contributing to a more secure environment for all.

Finally, prioritizing a robust incident response plan is crucial for mitigating damage when a cyberattack occurs. Companies should frequently test and refine their incident response protocols, ensuring that all relevant stakeholders know their roles and responsibilities. Regular simulations can help prepare teams for real-world scenarios, enabling a more coordinated and effective response when faced with actual threats. As organizations move toward 2025, being adaptable, informed, and proactive in risk management will prove essential in navigating the complexities of the ever-evolving cybersecurity landscape.

13. Collaboration in Cybersecurity

13.1 The Role of Information Sharing Platforms

Information sharing has become a cornerstone in addressing the rising threats posed by cybercrime and other malicious activities. The landscape of cybersecurity is constantly evolving, and professionals must understand that sharing insights and experiences can significantly strengthen defenses. The importance of this exchange lies in its ability to highlight vulnerabilities, track emerging threats, and foster a collective response that no single organization could achieve alone. By sharing crucial information, organizations can better prepare themselves against attacks, streamline incident recovery, and develop strategies that benefit everyone in their sector. The culture of sharing can also promote trust and collaboration, enabling entities to focus resources more effectively and anticipate future threats with greater accuracy.

Evaluating various information sharing platforms reveals a wide range of functionalities and effectiveness. Platforms such as Information Sharing and Analysis Centers (ISACs) have gained traction by providing structured communication channels for sharing critical threat intelligence in real time. Their ability to aggregate data from various industries ensures that even smaller businesses can benefit from insights typically reserved for larger companies with more resources. Other platforms, like Threat Exchanges and collaborative cybersecurity frameworks, offer users tools to analyze and disseminate information efficiently while maintaining privacy and security. However, challenges remain, such as ensuring data accuracy and the willingness of individuals and organizations to share sensitive information. The effectiveness of these platforms often hinges on user engagement and trust, meaning a successful model aligns technical capabilities with a community-centric approach.

In today's interconnected world, the key to strengthening cybersecurity lies not just in advanced technology, but in fostering a culture of information sharing. Professionals should actively seek out partnerships and collaborations, attending forums or workshops dedicated to these practices. Investing time in building relationships with others in the field can lead to richer, more actionable intelligence and a proactive stance against cyber threats. Regularly engaging with information sharing platforms also allows cybersecurity professionals to stay informed about the latest trends and vulnerabilities that may emerge as technology continues to evolve.

13.2 Building Strategic Alliances for Cyber Defense

In the realm of cybersecurity, the ever-evolving threat landscape necessitates a shift from isolated defense mechanisms to a more integrated approach through strategic alliances. Collaborative frameworks, such as the Cybersecurity Information Sharing Act (CISA) and initiatives spearheaded by organizations like the World Economic Forum, emphasize the importance of sharing intelligence, resources, and expertise among different entities. These alliances can take various forms, ranging from public-private partnerships to international coalitions. By leveraging shared data and collective experience, organizations can enhance their threat detection capabilities, streamline incident response, and foster a culture of continuous improvement across the cybersecurity community.

Building these alliances requires the establishment of trust and mutual benefits among all stakeholders. Effective communication and collaboration platforms are essential, enabling partners to exchange insights while preserving confidentiality and security. The establishment of standard operating procedures for information exchange, along with clearly defined roles, strengthens these partnerships. As organizations prepare for the challenges of 2025, embracing a collaborative mindset will be critical in creating a robust cybersecurity posture capable of adapting to new threats.

Numerous success stories illustrate the power of collaboration in enhancing cyber defense strategies. One notable example is the partnership between the U.S. Department of Homeland Security (DHS) and the private sector through its Cybersecurity and Infrastructure Security Agency (CISA). This collaboration facilitated the rapid sharing of threat intelligence during significant cyber events, such as the SolarWinds attack. By providing resources and real-time updates, CISA was able to assist affected organizations in implementing defensive measures swiftly, demonstrating the effectiveness of strategic alliances in mitigating harm.

Another compelling case is the collaboration between the Financial Services Information Sharing and Analysis Center (FS-ISAC) and various financial institutions. Through shared threat intelligence, banks and financial organizations can collectively identify vulnerabilities, confirm cyber threat occurrences, and respond more efficiently to threats. These partnerships not only reduce the impact of cyber attacks but also foster a proactive stance towards emerging threats by investing in training and resilience measures.

As organizations look towards 2025, the necessity for collaborative approaches in cybersecurity cannot be overstated. Establishing strategic alliances and learning from successful collaborations will empower entities to build a more resilient cyber ecosystem. Cybersecurity professionals are encouraged to actively engage with potential partners in their industry, share resources, and participate in initiatives that promote collective defense strategies, ultimately leading to a safer digital environment for everyone.

13.3 Encouraging Public-Private Partnerships

Public-private partnerships (PPPs) have emerged as a vital framework for addressing cybersecurity challenges. Different models of these partnerships can be tailored to suit diverse needs, providing a foundation for collaborative efforts. In a co-development model, both public entities and private organizations jointly create cybersecurity solutions. This not only pools resources but also leverages the specialized knowledge each party brings to the table, facilitating the development of more robust systems. Another effective model is the risk-sharing approach, where both sectors share the financial implications of cyber threats. By distributing the risk, organizations can better focus on innovative prevention and response strategies without bearing the entire burden alone. The intelligence-sharing model is also gaining traction, allowing public agencies to provide vital threat information to private firms while also receiving insights from their operational experiences. This mutual exchange enhances situational awareness and collective defense strategies, creating an effective shield against evolving cyber threats. As these models evolve and more organizations engage in PPPs, maintaining a clear line of communication and mutual trust is crucial for their success.

Collaboration through public-private partnerships in cybersecurity presents numerous advantages that can significantly bolster defenses against cyber threats. One prominent benefit is resource pooling. By combining financial, technological, and human resources, both public and private entities can implement more comprehensive security measures than they could achieve alone. This collaboration also fosters innovation, as diverse stakeholders bring different perspectives and capabilities to the table. Sharing knowledge, techniques, and technologies leads to the development of cutting-edge solutions tailored to emerging threats. Moreover, partnerships help build a coordinated response framework, allowing organizations to respond more effectively during incidents. This connection not only streamlines response efforts but also ensures that best practices are shared and replicated across sectors. With increased partnership, stakeholders can build upon each other's successes and learn from failures, ultimately creating a more resilient cybersecurity landscape. Engaging in these collaborative efforts also helps raise overall awareness of cybersecurity issues across various industries, encouraging proactive measures that benefit society as a whole.

Establishing effective public-private partnerships requires a commitment to ongoing dialogue and flexibility. Stakeholders should work together to identify shared goals and create strategic frameworks that adapt over time. Success hinges on understanding the importance of cultivating a culture of collaboration, where information security is viewed as a shared responsibility rather than a siloed endeavour. Practical tips for ensuring fruitful partnerships include hosting regular workshops to facilitate communication, establishing clear protocols for information sharing, and utilizing technology platforms that can securely connect partners. By fostering an environment built on trust and transparency, organizations can enhance their ability to navigate the complex landscape of cybersecurity threats, paving the way for future innovations.

14. Future Cybersecurity Products and Services

14.1 Anticipating Trends in Cybersecurity Tools

As the world moves into 2025, the landscape of cybersecurity continues to evolve rapidly. Emerging tools are setting the stage for more advanced practices that promise to enhance security protocols across various sectors. One notable advancement is the integration of artificial intelligence and machine learning into cybersecurity frameworks. These technologies are being developed to not only identify threats but also to learn from previous incidents, allowing for proactive measures rather than reactive ones. These AI-driven systems can analyze vast amounts of data in real-time, identifying patterns that human analysts might miss, and offering adaptive responses to cyber threats. Furthermore, tools that utilize behavioural analytics are becoming increasingly sophisticated, providing deeper insights into user patterns and potential anomalies that could indicate a breach. Additionally, the rise of quantum computing is anticipated to revolutionize encryption methods. While still in its infancy, quantum technology promises to create unbreakable encryption standards, substantially enhancing the way data is protected.

Despite the promising advancements, cybersecurity professionals face significant challenges when it comes to integrating new tools into their existing systems. One of the primary obstacles is compatibility with legacy systems, which many organizations still rely on. New tools and technologies often require substantial updates or complete overhauls of current infrastructure, which can be costly and time-consuming. Additionally, there is often a steep learning curve associated with adopting new technologies; employees may need extensive training to utilize these tools effectively, and resistance to change can hinder implementation efforts. Moreover, organizations must consider the continuity of security protocols during transitions, as any lapse could expose them to vulnerabilities. Compliance with regulatory standards also adds another layer of complexity, as companies must ensure that any new tools meet stringent security requirements. Addressing these integration challenges requires a strategic approach that balances innovation with practicality, ensuring that new tools enhance rather than hinder overall cybersecurity efforts.

For cybersecurity professionals looking forward to 2025, staying informed about emerging tools and understanding the intricacies of systems integration will be key. Fostering a culture of adaptability within teams can facilitate smoother transitions and encourage proactive engagement with new technologies.

14.2 The Growth of Managed Security Services

The managed services landscape has seen a remarkable transformation in recent years, particularly with the rise of Managed Security Service Providers (MSSPs). Today, organizations face ever-growing threats from cyberattacks that can disrupt operations and compromise sensitive data. MSSPs have emerged as a vital resource for many businesses in addressing these challenges. They offer tailored security solutions that are designed to protect against a wide range of vulnerabilities and threats. As cyber threats continue to evolve, the versatility and expertise of MSSPs empower organizations to adopt proactive security measures rather than merely reacting to incidents as they arise. This shift towards managed security services reflects a broader trend of businesses recognizing that cybersecurity is not just an IT issue but a critical component of overall business strategy.

When it comes to selecting an MSSP, organizations must carefully evaluate their options to find a provider that aligns with their specific needs and objectives. The evaluation process should consider several factors, including the MSSP's experience, technological capabilities, and the breadth of their service offerings. It's crucial to understand the MSSP's approach to cybersecurity, especially in terms of threat detection, incident response, and compliance management. Organizations should also assess the provider's ability to scale services effectively as their needs grow and change. Strong communication and transparency are vital, as a successful partnership hinges on the MSSP's ability to keep organizations informed about emerging threats and the overall effectiveness of the security strategy in place. Engaging with current clients of the MSSP can also provide valuable insights into their service quality and responsiveness.

As the cybersecurity landscape continues to mature, organizations that leverage MSSPs are likely to see benefits that extend beyond enhanced security. Embracing managed security services enables companies to focus on core business operations while experts handle their security needs. This strategic partnership not only fortifies defenses but also ensures that organizations remain agile and competitive in an increasingly complex digital landscape. For businesses looking to move forward, investing in the right MSSP can significantly enhance their security posture and preparedness for future threats. When evaluating providers, always ask about their incident response times and proactive measures. This insight can prove invaluable in ensuring comprehensive protection against the continuously evolving threat landscape.

14.3 Innovations in Endpoint Protection Solutions

The landscape of endpoint protection technologies continues to evolve rapidly, with new innovations emerging to keep pace with increasingly sophisticated cyber threats. One of the most significant advancements is the integration of artificial intelligence (AI) and machine learning (ML) into endpoint security solutions. These technologies enable systems to proactively detect anomalies and potential threats by analyzing vast amounts of data in real-time. AI-driven solutions can assess user behaviour, identify unusual patterns, and respond to potential breaches much faster than traditional methods. Additionally, the automation of incident responses helps organizations mitigate risks more efficiently, allowing them to focus resources on more strategic tasks. Another exciting innovation is the rise of Extended Detection and Response (XDR) technologies, which unify security across various platforms and endpoints. XDR provides a holistic view of the security landscape and enhances collaboration among different security tools, making the detection and response processes more cohesive.

As we look towards future threats, it becomes essential to strategize how endpoint protection can rise to the occasion. Ransomware continues to be a major concern, and organizations need to prepare by investing in robust backup solutions and maintaining strict access controls. Implementing a zero-trust model can significantly enhance security; this strategy ensures that no one is trusted by default, regardless of whether they are inside or outside the network perimeter. Regularly updating software and applying security patches are pivotal in defending against exploit-driven attacks. Furthermore, continuous employee training on cybersecurity protocols helps build a security-conscious culture within organizations, making them less vulnerable to phishing and social engineering tactics. Considering the stratospheric growth of IoT devices, ensuring these endpoints are adequately secured is critical. Strategies such as device isolation and robust authentication mechanisms for IoT devices can mitigate the unique risks they introduce.

Staying ahead in the rapidly changing world of endpoint protection requires a commitment to continuous improvement and adaptation. Cybersecurity professionals should prioritize developing an agile strategy that incorporates evolving technologies and accommodates emerging threats. Regular vulnerability assessments and penetration testing will provide insights into potential weaknesses, informing more effective security measures. Emphasizing collaboration across departments can lead to more comprehensive security strategies that benefit the entire organization. By fostering a proactive security posture and embracing innovative technologies, organizations can effectively safeguard their networks and data against future challenges.

15. Preparing for the Unexpected

15.1 Scenario Planning for Emerging Threats

Scenario planning has become crucial for organizations facing the unpredictability of modern cyber threats. As the landscape of cybercrime evolves, the ability to prepare for unforeseen incidents is no longer a luxury but a necessity. The value in scenario planning lies in its capacity to provide organizations with a framework for understanding potential threats, allowing them to build resilience and a more robust security posture. By envisioning various threat scenarios, cybersecurity professionals can identify gaps in their current defenses, mobilize resources more effectively, and ensure that their teams are not just reacting but are prepared to respond proactively to emerging risks. The ever-changing nature of technology, including advancements in artificial intelligence and the shift to more interconnected systems, poses an ongoing risk that requires continuous re-evaluation of security strategies.

Developing effective scenarios is essential for maximizing the benefits of scenario planning. Best practices involve a thorough analysis of existing vulnerabilities and threats, incorporating insights from industry trends and intelligence reports. Engaging a broad range of stakeholders, from executive leadership to technical teams, ensures that varying perspectives are considered and enhances the relevance of the scenarios created. It's important for cybersecurity organizations to include both plausible and extreme scenarios in their planning. This exercise encourages teams to think creatively about the potential impacts and to devise innovative strategies to mitigate risks. Regularly updating these scenarios ensures they remain relevant in the face of rapidly changing circumstances, while tabletop exercises and simulations provide practical experience and reveal potential weaknesses in response plans.

The insights gained from scenario planning can significantly influence an organization's strategic security decisions. By effectively anticipating future threats, organizations can allocate their budget and personnel towards areas of greatest concern, improving their overall readiness. Collaboration and communication are key throughout this process; sharing insights with peers in the industry can lead to more nuanced understandings of threat landscapes and shared best practices. A practical tip for cybersecurity professionals is to set aside time quarterly to review scenario plans and adapt them based on the latest threat intelligence. This proactive approach ensures that preparedness becomes ingrained in the corporate culture, fostering an environment where security is everyone's responsibility.

15.2 The Impact of Global Events on Cybersecurity

Global events serve as significant catalysts for shifts in cybersecurity incidents and trends. The interconnectedness of our world means that events such as natural disasters, political unrest, and major public health crises can trigger a surge in cyber threats. For instance, during the COVID-19 pandemic, cybercriminals exploited the confusion and fear surrounding the virus, leveraging phishing campaigns and malware designed to mimic health advisories and government guidelines. This trend illustrates how physical and economic disruptions can lead to a ripe environment for cyber exploitation.

Moreover, geopolitical events, such as tensions between nations or international conflicts, often lead to increased cyber warfare activities. State-sponsored attacks can escalate as countries seek to gain a strategic advantage or undermine rivals. Examples include ransomware attacks targeting critical infrastructure, which can leave entire cities vulnerable. The subsequent data breaches not only have immediate repercussions for the affected organizations but can also impact national security, creating a layered complexity that cybersecurity professionals must navigate. With global events continually evolving, maintaining vigilance against potential threats is paramount.

In light of the ever-changing landscape shaped by global events, organizations need to proactively adapt their security strategies. One effective approach is to conduct regular risk assessments that take into account potential external threats linked to current events. Assessing vulnerabilities in the context of global developments allows companies to prioritize their cybersecurity measures and allocate resources effectively. For instance, if a region experiences political instability, organizations operating in that area should enhance their monitoring and protection protocols against potential data breaches.

Another essential strategy is to foster a culture of cybersecurity awareness within the organization. Providing ongoing training for employees about recognizing phishing attempts and other social engineering tactics can significantly reduce the risk of successful attacks. Organizations should also invest in advanced technologies such as artificial intelligence and machine learning that can detect anomalies in network behaviour, offering an additional layer of defense. Moreover, developing robust incident response plans that incorporate lessons learned from past global events helps organizations to respond quickly and effectively when incidents occur. Keeping abreast of global trends and continuously adapting security measures is crucial for staying one step ahead of cyber threats.

As global events continue to unfold, staying updated on emerging trends and threats in cybersecurity is vital for both organizations and professionals. Subscribing to relevant cybersecurity threat intelligence feeds can provide insights into the current landscape and help prepare for potential threats. This practice allows organizations to refine their strategies and respond proactively to new challenges as they arise.

15.3 Fostering Resilience in Cybersecurity Strategies

Cybersecurity is evolving rapidly, and fostering resilience is becoming essential for organizations. Resilience in cybersecurity means being prepared for, responding to, and recovering from cyber incidents effectively. The foundation of building resilience lies in several key principles that organizations must adopt as part of their cybersecurity strategies. First, organizations should shift their focus from purely preventive measures to a more holistic approach that includes detection, response, and recovery. This means integrating tools and practices that not only prevent attacks but also allow for quick detection of threats and efficient recovery processes. Continuous monitoring and real-time threat intelligence play crucial roles in this adaptive strategy.

Another vital principle is the importance of a robust incident response plan. This plan should detail specific roles and responsibilities during an incident, ensuring that every team member knows how to act. Regular drills and simulations can keep employees sharp and prepared, fostering a culture of resilience within the organization. Additionally, investing in training and awareness programs will prepare staff at all levels to recognize potential threats, thus reducing the likelihood of human error during critical moments. This cultural shift toward security awareness not only empowers individuals but also enhances the organization's overall security posture.

Several organizations have exemplified effective resilience in their cybersecurity practices, serving as models for others. One notable case is a major financial institution that faced a significant cyber attack. Rather than becoming overwhelmed, they executed their well-practiced incident response plan, swiftly isolating affected systems to prevent further damage. Their emphasis on training and awareness allowed their employees to recognize phishing attempts, significantly reducing the initial breach's impact. By implementing continuous learning and adapting their strategies in real-time based on attack patterns, this institution not only mitigated the attack's effects but emerged stronger with enhanced security measures.

Another example can be seen in a tech startup that prioritized resilience from its inception. By incorporating security into their DevOps processes, they encouraged a collaborative approach between development and security teams. This practice facilitated a rapid response to vulnerabilities as they were discovered, minimizing potential impacts. Additionally, they maintained an agile framework that allowed them to pivot and adapt their strategies as new threats emerged. Their proactive stance on cybersecurity made them less vulnerable compared to competitors who viewed security as an afterthought, showcasing how resilience can provide a competitive advantage in a volatile cyber landscape.

Emphasizing resilience in cybersecurity isn't just about defending against threats; it's about becoming agile and adaptable in the face of adversity. Organizations can glean much from these examples by understanding that resilience is not a one-time effort but an ongoing journey that requires consistent evaluation and adaptation.